THE HISTORY OF THE HAMMOCK
Including historical information on Fort Drum & Okeechobee

Welcome to
the Hammock
Carol Devine

I thank all of the members who took time to speak to me about their memories, provided documents, and shared their photographs. Your assistance has made this possible.

Table of Contents

PART ONE

The History of Indian Hammock

CHAPTER ONE
In the Beginning
...and the Land Was Without Form

What was here before the roads, the houses, the pastures? Who conceived this and who put into action the idea of keeping a little bit of old Florida tucked away in a modern world? When and how did all of this happen? Put on your boots and come with me as we begin our look back at the history of Indian Hammock Hunt and Riding Club.

To best understand how everything came about, we first go back to the early 1900's Fort Drum. After the Florida East Coast Railroad (FEC) built the railways and the Fort Drum depot, this area was active in the cypress timbering business. The land where we now live was once rich with cypress trees. A portion of the railroad even ran across the northeast section of the property. Load upon load of timber was sent out via the rails each week.

The dream of an area that would capture and hold onto a little bit of old Florida was conceived by a visionary man named Al J. Cone. Mr. Cone was a fifth-generation Floridian whose grandfather worked here in the cypress timbering industry. Mr. Cone loved the area and wished to preserve it for future generations. When Mr. Cone graduated from University of Florida in 1943, the United States was at war in both the Pacific and across the Atlantic.

Mr. Cone delayed his entrance to law school and went on to serve in Europe with the Army's 102nd Infantry Division, earning a Silver Star and several Purple Hearts. At the completion of his service, he returned to the University of Florida and completed law school. At his West Palm Beach law practice, he specialized in personal injury litigation, where Mr. Cone built a reputation as one of the nation's leading trial lawyers.

In the 1970's, he returned to the Fort Drum area to begin to put his dream into action. The area where his grandfather had worked in cypress timbering was now a pine tree and tomato farm owned by the family of the late Dr. Charles Sample. About 1000 acres were dedicated to the pine trees with the tomato farming area in the spot we now call the "outback". He established a corporation known as Indian Hammock Enterprises, Inc., which was incorporated as a Domestic For-Profit Corporation on July 2, 1973. The listed corporate officers were Al Cone, Imogene Cone (his wife), and friend and another fifth generation Floridian, TJ Durrance.

With the property now under the corporate ownership, Gee & Jenson Engineers-Architects-Planners, Inc. of West Palm Beach was contracted to plat the 299 residential lots, roadways, and common areas. They were also charged with obtaining the necessary approvals from the Florida Land Sales Board so that lot sales could begin.

Since the initial purchase did not include the first one mile directly west of Highway 441, the entrance to Indian Hammock was initially off of the west end of 325th Trail.

This entrance path connected to Indian Hammock Trail approximately one-third of a mile east of Cabbage Palm Court.

Aerial photo of original access route

Al Cone's dream is now becoming a reality. With platting underway and while still awaiting the state's Land Sales Board approval, Indian Hammock Hunt and Riding Club, Inc. was established as a not-for-profit Florida Corporation in the summer of 1973.

Advertising of the community was the next step for the Cones and Durrances. Although lot sales could not begin until they received Land Sales Board approval, the group got a jump-start on introducing this unique community to the public.

Since Al Cone was a member of the Florida Bar, he had easy access to the names and addresses of about 600 law colleagues in the South Florida area. He wisely started the marketing campaign with them. Bill Dover still remembers receiving his postcard back in 1973. Bill even recalls that it was blue. The postcard was an invitation to tour the property and join the Cones for a wild hog barbeque. Bill and the others who accepted the invitation were treated to a tasty meal in the picnic hammock under the granddaddy oak trees. That area, adjacent to the chapel, is still available today for picnics.

Bill recalled that after he dined on the wild hog, he was taken in a hunt buggy to tour some of the lots that would be the first released for sale. Although he was not able to make the purchase that day, he did reserve lots 55 and 56, where he resides fulltime today. Bill went on to say that although TJ Durrance drove the buggy and pointed out the two choice lots, it was his wife and realtor, Shirley Durrance, who excelled in sales.

Shirley Durrance on horseback

Al and Imogene Cone were also early lot owners, purchasing lot 53. They built their home on the lot in 1974 and were frequent weekend visitors. Also in 1974, Mr. Cone's law firm purchased lot 18 and built a cabin on the land, which was made available for weekends to the employees of the firm. Additionally, another law partner, Mr. Ward Wagner, was the original owner of lot 7.

With this section of Indian Hammock filled with lawyers, the history of the only street not named for wildlife or nature has become clearer. That street was aptly named, "Law Firm Lane".

Law Firm Lane street sign

Over the next two years, the Cones and Durrances continued their marketing plan of feeding potential buyers delicious barbeque on many weekends. Large quarter-page advertisements were placed frequently in the Palm Beach Post touting, "We have the answer to inflation, Indian Hammock Hunt and Riding Club, Inc." Lots were selling, but very slowly, much slower than Mr. Cone had anticipated, and it was time for action.

That action came in the form of a partnership with Connecticut Mutual Insurance Company of Glastonbury, Connecticut. The company's Agricultural Loan Group had a long history of funding agricultural projects. They were well-known for successfully funding projects around the United States with specialties in farmland, cattle ranches, and vineyards. During the Great Depression, Connecticut Mutual had the unique distinction of never foreclosing on any of the agricultural loans they funded. The vice president in charge of the Agricultural Loan Group in 1975 was Denzel Warden. Maria Wolf was his secretary.

With an action plan in place and after completing the appropriate paperwork, Connecticut Mutual Insurance Agricultural Group accepted Mr. Cone as a client. I discovered in my research that in 1973, Al Cone had established another corporation, Indian Hammock Ranch Estates, Inc. Whereas Indian Hammock Enterprises, Inc. was the corporation of record for the initial purchase of the land from Dr. Sample's family, Indian Hammock Ranch Estates, Inc. was the corporation of record for the ongoing development of the community and the lot sales. Mr. Cone was listed as the first president of Indian Hammock Ranch Estates, Inc., as well as remaining president of Indian Hammock Enterprises, Inc. Indian Hammock Ranch Estates was the corporation that entered into the partnership with Connecticut Mutual. Then, in 1976, Indian Hammock Enterprises, Inc. was dissolved.

Al & Imogene Cone riding, 1973

...and the Land Brought Forth

Indian Hammock Hunt and Riding Club, Ltd., a limited partnership, was registered with the State of Florida on May 14, 1975. The original general partners were Indian Hammock Ranch Estates, Inc. and Mr. W. T. Cox. Mr. Cox (first name Willo), from Orlando, was the declared Resident Agent for Connecticut Mutual. Another Resident Agent working with Mr. Cox was Mr. Lake Coleman from the Mount Dora area.

A path north of the horse hospital, Willo Run, was named for Mr. Cox and, as you would expect, the lakeside picnic area called Lake Coleman was named for Mr. Coleman.

Willo Run street sign   *Lake Coleman directional sign*

With the partnership completed and filed with the state, it was time to get back to business. Besides lot sales, the partners now were actively designing, permitting, and building the first amenities, which included the lodge. The initial dream design of the lodge was that of a spacious hunting lodge in excess of 12,000 square feet. This design called for a two-story building with lodging rooms to rent on the second floor and a large lobby and dining room on the first floor.

None of the documents available and none of the early residents could shed light on why the lodge was downsized. However, logic would lead one to conclude that it was due to financial constraints.

Artist conception drawing of future lodge

When the lodge was completed in 1975, it consisted of the kitchen and dining room in one building and the bathrooms in another. Connecting the two buildings was a large open-air wood deck with the decking continuing behind the dining room.

In the late 1970's, with the partnership in force, the group filed for and received their licensure as a developer from the Florida Department of Professional and Business Regulation. With plenty of work to be done, the next step was to hire a maintenance staff. They hired a staff of three, which included Roger Brewer. The staff maintained the roads, worked on the improvements, and maintained the facilities. Roger also conducted trail rides on the weekends for the residents and their guests.

As weekend barbeques and lot marketing continued, more lots sold and the developer continued adding improvements. Besides the lodge, they installed the pool and tennis courts, built the cabana, tack room, cottage, bunkhouse, and hunt shack.

Additionally, in the late 70's, the developer purchased the area of land between US 441 and the turn where Indian Hammock Trail connected to 325th Trail. Indian Hammock Trail was extended eastward to 441, eliminating the need to use 325th Trail as the entrance. Shortly after the road was extended, the first gatehouse was constructed by the developer and was located on the north side of the entrance. Nancy Brewer was one of the first gate attendants in 1977. She recalled that Indian Hammock Trail was not as wide as it is now. She also explained that the "gate" that she "operated" was actually a rope strung across the entranceway that she dropped to the ground for the visitor to drive over when entering and exiting. Notice in the photo the original location and number of U.S. Post Office mailboxes.

First gatehouse

In 1979, the developer finally sold the minimum number of lots required by Florida law and set a date for community control to be transferred to the homeowners. A Liaison

Committee was established for the smooth transition of the property to the owners. The date of the transfer was set for October 28, 1979 at the annual members meeting. The agenda included the election of the first Board of Directors. All members received the announcement in the Hammock Herald, printed on two sheets of copier paper, published at the time by member John Pond.

At the 1979 annual members meeting, the transfer of the property was accomplished and the first Board of Directors was elected. The first board was set at nine directors with Bill Dover elected as the first president. Also, on that first board were names still familiar to everyone today, John Hume and Ed Foster. The first board established the fiscal year as November 1 to October 31, and retained Gary Moorman as the first auditor to oversee the financial transfer from the developer to the homeowners. This first board selected Mike Baker as part-time manager. His contract was set at six months with a salary of $1,500 per year and with accommodations on-site in Indian Hammock. Also at that meeting, approval was given to hire Roger Brewer as the first fulltime employee.

The Board of Directors managed the day-to-day activities of the community, supervised the employee(s), and handled the finances until finally, on February 15, 1981, the first fulltime manager position was budgeted. The manager's salary was set at $15,000 per year plus a $400 car allowance. On April 26, 1981, Armin Mayer was appointed as the first fulltime manager.

CHAPTER THREE
...and Darkness Was Upon the Land

A very dark year, 1981. The visions of progress and bright days were shattered in February of 1981 when the first major forest fire erupted. At that time, Indian Hammock was almost exclusively populated by weekenders. This fire occurred mid-week. Initially, the fire started as a grass fire at the north fence-line hunt area, but quickly spread, engulfing multiple lots in the area of Armadillo Avenue. Many of the lot owners were contacted to alert them of the fire and potential property loss. Bill Dover recalled being contacted at work, and still remembered that he was in a meeting when the call arrived. Bill was told that his house had likely burned to the ground. He quickly gathered Diane and the rest of the family and headed north, dreading what he was about to find. Upon arriving at the Indian Hammock entrance, he recalled the thick black smoke that still hovered and seemed to go on for miles. He and his family prepared for the worst as they continued the final approach to their lot, lot 56. Although all of the trees in the area were lost and the undergrowth of palmettos was scorched, the family was happy to find their home untouched by the fire. Thanks to the quick actions of the Indian Hammock employees, who were first to arrive with the one and only fire truck Indian Hammock had at that time, the county fire department, and Division of Forestry, no houses or lives were lost.

The Indian Hammock members' gratitude was evident at a special board meeting held on February 15. The board made and passed unanimously a motion to donate $1500 to the various firefighting agencies that helped extinguish the fire. With the memory of the fire fresh in all of the members' minds, a push toward fire safety and control was the new order of business. An additional fire truck was purchased and the idea of first responders took root. Additionally, the use of firebreaks was implemented.

Adding to the 1981 dark cloud was a fatal vehicle accident. Although not many of the details are available, the death of a female visitor to Indian Hammock was the result of a single car rollover accident. After litigation, Indian Hammock's insurance company settled the claim out of court for $1.4 million, of which the club was responsible for $52,000.

Indian Hammock members, however, did not lose heart. It was also in 1981 that a very special place was approved, the chapel. In June, the Chapel in the Woods, an "all faiths" chapel, found its home under the granddaddy oaks in the picnic hammock. It was a place for members to forget the troubles of 1981 and reflect on their future. The chapel today still serves as a place of happy celebrations, memorial memories, and quiet contemplation, where members can reflect on the blessings in their lives.

Although control of Indian Hammock had passed from the developer to the association in 1979, the developer still owned more than 80 lots. Assisting Indian Hammock Hunt and Riding Club, LTD (the developer's limited partnership) with their lot sales were members Frank Denise and Paul and Mary Hamm. Through the years since 1979, the partnership voted at the annual members meetings as owners of the unsold lots. It is noted in the board of directors meeting minutes that the partnership typically voted with the majority. This practice continued as the partnership slowly sold their remaining lots.

With the difficult year of 1981 behind them, the Indian Hammock members were very happy 1982 was relatively uneventful. Armin Mayer continued as property manager until November 30, 1982. After his resignation, the manager position was not filled; rather, the board of directors resumed the roll of handling the day-to-day business of the club. However, the board did approve the hiring of the first administrative secretary/bookkeeper. Filling this new position was Edith "Cookie" Lightsey, who received a starting salary of $220 per week plus mileage. Then, in April of 1983, she tendered her resignation with a departure date of September 30, 1983. Rather than hire a replacement for the upcoming vacancy, the board approved the purchase of a computerized accounting system to be used by Fleming, O'Bryan, and Fleming in Fort Lauderdale. The cost to Indian Hammock included purchasing the initial programing and a monthly fee for use of the equipment and the individual to enter the data.

In 1985, many unfortunate circumstances disrupted the community's peace, and culminated with a major change at the January 1986 members meeting. The upheavals of 1985 began with the multiple changes of the board meeting schedules. At the beginning of 1985, the monthly meetings were held at the lodge on Sunday mornings at 9 am. In March, the meetings were moved to Friday nights at 9 pm. Then in August, they returned to Sunday at 9 am, quickly changing to Sunday at 8 am for the September meeting. Then in October, the meeting was held on Saturday at 1 pm.

In November, the meeting again returned to Friday night at 9 pm. The final meeting of 1985 was held at 5 pm on Saturday, December 14.

It was also during 1985 that most, possibly all, of the lots that the partnership owned were sold. In September of 1985, members Mary and Paul Hamm assisted the partnership with the sale of 75 lots to then member Frank Cerchiaro, who bought them as an investment. Mr. Cerchiaro planned to sell the lots by auction. At the October 1985 board meeting, Mr. Frank Denise made the announcement of the multi-lot purchase and of the pending auction that was scheduled for November 16, 1985. The auction company handling the sale was Higgenbotham and the sale was being held on Indian Hammock property. Mr. Denise and the Hamms worked with Mr. Cerchiaro to oversee the auction.

The Indian Hammock membership was not happy that the lots would be sold in this manner and there was concern that the sale would decrease property values. As the days to the auction approached, the tension in the community rose considerably. The auction was being held under a tent erected near the lodge. At one point, a member roped off the entrance to the lodge to block potential bidders from wandering into our lodge. Manny and Gail MacLain had been looking for property with an airstrip and responded to the announcement they had received in the mail. They were one of the buyers on the day of the auction.

On the day of the auction, the bidders descended on Indian Hammock. Gail MacLain recalled, with remarkable detail, how the day went. She explained that a tent was set up in the area where the campers enter near the lodge. The bidders were able to go from the front gate to the tent, where they were met by Paul Hamm. A large map of Indian Hammock was posted in the tent with the available lots highlighted. Paul Hamm then offered a tour of the community via his personal vehicle. Once the visitors selected the lot(s) they wanted to bid on, the auction began. Gail and Manny won the bid on the second and third lots that came up for auction. Although 75 lots were scheduled for auction, the auction was halted after the 5th sale. Gail did not recall who stopped the auction or the specific reason why; however, it was possibly due to low sale prices. At the conclusion of the auction, the winners of the five lots were required to provide the seller with three reference letters: one from their bank, one from their employer, and one reference letter from a member.

Although tension remained high, no one was ready for what transpired two months later at the January 1986 members meeting. As always, it was time to vote for a new board of directors. A proxy system was in place for members who could not attend the meeting. At 9 am, the meeting was called to order by President John Hume and a quorum was established. It was then that the membership in attendance was notified that Paul Hamm held 97 votes including proxies, and Frank Denise held 69 votes including proxies. After six of the proxies were disqualified, the total votes held by the two members was 161. The remaining 88 votes were represented by individuals or proxies to John Hume, Bill Dover, and Ed Foster. Forty-four lots were not represented.

The first motion of the meeting was made by Paul Hamm reducing the number of directors from 13 to 5. The motion was seconded by Frank Denise and passed with the 161 votes of Hamm and Denise. The remaining members did not cast their votes.

The second motion was from George Abraham who moved that the meeting be adjourned. The motion was seconded, but was defeated by the 161 votes of Hamm and Denise. After several candidates withdrew from the election, the members who were up for consideration were: John Hume, Al Iosue, Joan Powell, Dottie Westby, Paul Hamm, Mary Hamm, Frank Denise, and George Abraham.

The new board of five members was elected with 161 votes. They were Paul Hamm, Mary Hamm, Frank Denise, John Hume, and Dottie Westby. As before, the other members did not cast their votes. The meeting was adjourned at 10 am with the members still in shock over what had just occurred.

Both former and current members described their feelings about that meeting. Bill Dover, who was on the 1985 board, recalled feeling angry and recalled that his co-directors were also angry. Another member recalled that those not selected to the new board walked out of the meeting. Gail MacLain, who had been a member for two short months, wondered "why the heck we bought here". John Hume remembered having high expectations of many new members being in attendance and was disappointed when they were not. Dottie Westby remembered that Paul Hamm was hoping to make things calm and return Indian Hammock to the simple life it had been in the beginning.

Corky Walker, former member and then lodge committee chair, recalled that Paul Hamm wanted to take the job of manager and wanted his wife to be the secretary/bookkeeper. Corky also remembered that the members were not in agreement with his plan.

At the conclusion of the 1986 members meeting, the January board of directors meeting was called to order, and the new board of five began the meeting by electing officers. The president was Paul Hamm, vice president was Mary Hamm, and the secretary was Dottie Westby, with the position of treasurer unfilled until the February 1986 meeting, when John Hume accepted the position.

The board was set at five; however, several of the members were working together to find a way to return the board to 13. The process involved the structuring of another corporation. Hammock Associates, Inc. was incorporated with the State of Florida in March of 1986. Frank Cerchiaro joined members Bill Dover, Ed Foster, and several others, and pooled their resources to purchase the remaining 60 lots in the corporate name.

The directors of Hammock Associates, Inc. were Frank Cerchiaro, president, and Ed Foster, secretary. The first order of business for the corporation was to complete the sale of the 60 remaining lots from Frank Cerchiaro into the name of Hammock Associates, Inc. The closing on the lots occurred on March 27, 1986, just one day after the corporation was registered with the state.

Two days later, a special board meeting was held on March 29, 1986. Dottie Westby motioned that a special members meeting be held in May to re-establish a 13-member board and elect eight new directors. The motion was seconded by Mary Hamm and passed unanimously.

At 11 am on May 10, 1986, the special members meeting was held in the lodge. Unfortunately, the minutes from that meeting are not available, so the specific votes cast for reinstating a 13-member board are unavailable. However, the board of directors did meet at 1:30 that same day and eight new board members were identified as: Bill Dover, Ed Foster, Al Iosue, Jim Lassiter, Joan Powell, Frank Rich, Bob Walker, and Steve Rehak.

The first order of business for the new board was to accept Frank Denise's resignation from the board. The vacant position was immediately filled with the appointment of Bill LaDue. With a 13-member board reinstated, a motion was made and passed to remove all officers from their positions. John Hume was appointed chair of the meeting, pending the selection of a president. The officers were then elected as follows: Al Iosue, president; Bob Walker, first vice-president; Frank Rich, second vice-president; John Hume, treasurer; and Steve Rehak, secretary. Paul and Mary Hamm were not re-elected as officers, but remained on the board.

With the board returned to thirteen and new officers elected, the remainder of the meeting returned to business as usual with committees announced, and new members and building plans approved.

At the June meeting, Paul and Mary Hamm resigned from the board. Member and former manager, Armin Mayer, was added to the board at the July meeting bringing the total number of directors to 12 for the remainder of 1986.

The July meeting also reversed the meeting day upheaval of the previous year. It was at this meeting that the board decided to hold all future board meetings on the third Sunday of the month at 9 am.

The board activities for the remainder of the year included: beginning the first draft of the rules and regulations, starting the search for a fulltime manager, approving an archery range located northwest of the lodge, and overseeing the construction of a new equipment barn/office by Cowboy Raulerson.

CHAPTER FOUR
Let There Be Light

With 1986 behind them, it was time for Indian Hammock to get back to some fun times. This was a place for the weekend residents to escape the stresses of everyday life.

Trail rides had been a constant for the community since the developer used trail rides as an enticement when courting new lot buyers. The ownership of the developer's horses was transferred to the club in 1979 and staff was retained to direct the trail rides at a modest cost as a recreational amenity. When the insurer refused to renew the club's liability policy in 1987, a self-insurance program was adopted to keep the trail riding activity available. The consensus was that Indian Hammock, even by virtue of its name, was a "riding club" and that it was important to maintain this amenity for the residents.

I spoke to Corky Walker, a former longtime member. As you may recall, Corky was the Lodge Committee chair and was in charge of special events. Corky shed some light on some of the activities that were available at that time.

First, she explained that the large deck surrounding the lodge had two large fire pits. The fire pits were lit every weekend and made available to the members for grilling their meals. Those members who wished could come to the lodge with their grilling selection and prepare their meal with their neighbors. Corky recalls many nights that there would be over 100 people grilling, fellowshipping, and just enjoying the tranquility that Indian Hammock offers. Corky also explained that they had many themed parties. She recalled a square dance and a casino night, just to name a few. On

November 14, 1987, the Lodge Committee hosted a "Country Fair" as a fundraiser, netting $2220 that was used to fund future parties and events.

Maintaining the woods was also on the minds of the early residents, so much so that an Ecology Committee was formed. The committee was assigned a designated area of common land on which to cultivate a plant nursery. After preparing the land, trees and bushes were planted and harvested by these hard-working committee members. The benefit to the Hammock was twofold. The committee transplanted the trees onto common areas where the pine beetle had ravished the foliage, and the trees were made available for purchase by members for only five dollars each.

Although the board had been actively looking for a manager for almost a year, none was found to be suitable. The board halted their search in August of 1987 and initiated a Management Committee consisting of three members. The committee was responsible for the day-to-day activities of the community and oversaw the employees. They reported updates directly to board of directors at monthly meetings.

In December of 1987, our swimming pool was the site used by the Fort Drum Community Church for their baptisms.

During 1988, Hammock Associates, Inc. began discussions with a Boca Raton developer who believed he could sell the remaining lots to individuals interested in polo. The board tentatively approved the concept of a 25-acre parcel beside the airstrip as the future polo grounds. The lot sales to the developer were never completed; thus, no polo grounds were needed. However, on November 19 and 20, the community was treated to a polo demonstration that was held on the airstrip. The polo players were accompanied by about 10 ladies dressed for the day in their fancy polo attire including brimmed hats. Some tables were set up on the sidelines and champagne was served to the guests.

A trail ride and picnic were also hosted that weekend. The trail riders started and ended at the lodge where all attending enjoyed a country picnic.

As the 1980's come to a close, Indian Hammock continues to blossom. In 1989, the yet unnamed building near the Skeet and Trap field was completed. The building was funded by a bank loan secured by a first mortgage on the 330 acres of land at the entrance to the club. The amount needed to complete the building was $18,200. Once constructed, the building was named the Bird's Nest by then-member Walter Jolly. The loan was actually thousands more than the $18,200 so that funds were available for a new gatehouse, an equipment barn, and renovations to the lodge.

It was also in 1989 that the Post Office notified the board the mailboxes were not acceptable for mail delivery and that the post office would no longer deliver mail to the individual boxes. This resulted in all of the community mail being delivered to the gate. The gate staff was then charged with the task of sorting the mail and placing it in the mailboxes. Fortunately, most members did not use their Indian Hammock address as their mailing address.

The Ecology Committee continued successfully cultivating trees and, in keeping with the board's philanthropic heart, six trees were donated to the Fort Drum Community Church and six more to Okeechobee Elementary School.

In December of 1989, the bids went out for the renovation of the lodge. At the July 1990 board meeting, the vote was unanimous to award the renovation project to Ron Maggion.

Even though the club had adopted a self-insurance plan for liability coverage for the trail rides, by January 1990 the club was unable to continue to fund the amenity. Rather than just discontinue trail rides altogether, the board worked diligently seeking a viable alternative.

By March of 1990, after polling the membership to determine the level of interest for a "saddle club", 12 members expressed their desire to join. Then, in May 1990, those 12 members became the first members of the saddle club, which was given the official name of Remuda Club. Remuda is defined in the dictionary as: "a herd of horses that have been saddle-broken, from which ranch hands choose their mounts for the day". Thanks to the hard work of the board and the members who paid a small annual fee to join the club, Indian Hammock continued to live up to its name, "riding club".

Also, exciting news for 1990 was the installation of lights at the airstrip. This would allow for the pilots to fly in on Friday night rather than waiting until Saturday morning. Dr. Thomas Breza proposed to the board the initial concept, whereby, he would donate the materials needed and volunteers would complete the installation. The board approved the plan and, a short time later, lights lined the airstrip for after-dark use.

Prior to 1990, the entire area between Persimmon Tree Lane and Blue Heron Lane, south of Indian Hammock Trail, was dedicated to a cattle lease. In June of 1990, the area was split, with the easternmost half continuing as the cattle lease and the western portion authorized as a recreation area. This new park-like area was named the Edward T. Foster Recreation Area in honor of Ed Foster for his unending support of Indian Hammock. The T-shaped lake on that property, formerly known simply as T-Lake, was also renamed as Foster Lake. I spoke to Barbara Hume this week who spoke highly of Ed Foster and stated, "I don't know where Indian Hammock would be without all of his support. Ed was always ready to help and never hesitated to write a check."

Indian Hammock's first employee, Roger Brewer, and his family resided in the bunkhouse during many years of his employment with the maintenance department. Then in 1990, the board authorized the purchase of a used trailer to house another full-time staff member. The trailer was located near the front gate on the south side of Indian Hammock Trail and, over the years, was home to several different employees. These residences were offered to the employees rent-free as part of their compensation package.

To finish 1990, Indian Hammock purchased their first computer. The model chosen was an IBM XT 36 PC. The $4200 purchase price included software, printer, and power pack.

The members meeting of 1991 was the first election needed since 1986. In the years prior, 1987 through 1990, the total number of candidates running was 13. In each of those four years, the board was appointed by acclamation. Finally, in 1991, 16 members put their hat in the ring for a spot on the board requiring the membership cast ballots.

In August of 1991, the board approved the purchase of the first fax machine for the office and allocated $500 for the purchase.

In November, the 1992 budget was submitted and approved. The budget maintained the monthly assessment fee per lot at $85.00.

The year 1992 brought some new ideas and fun for the members. Starting on March 14, 1992, the first firearms safety course was conducted by member, Lew Whiting. Classes continued on a monthly basis with many members in attendance. Then in April of 1992, improvements to Foster Recreation Area were approved in concept. The improvements included two holes of pasture golf, a tiki hut, additional trees for shade, and picnic tables.

Also in April, Ed Foster announced that Hammock Associates, Inc. had sold their last lot. He also announced that a "SOLD OUT" celebration would be held at the lodge later in the summer.

Even with all of the good news, there was bad news to be shared. Vandalism was a big problem that year. Multiple areas of the Hammock were involved, including the skeet and trap range, rifle pistol range, stables, and the Chapel, where the altar was overturned and several pews uprooted. A security committee was in place at that time and everyone was encouraged to report any further problems to the committee.

Another issue that year involved members failing to lock the front gate in the evenings after entering or leaving. This behavior led to a bounty system being established. Any member or employee who provided the board with information and the name of the violator would be paid a $50 bounty for their report. The first bounty paid was in April of 1992 to Roger Brewer and the violator was fined by the board $100.

Things around Indian Hammock continued to be busy throughout the spring and summer of 1992. The flurry of activity started with the First Annual Skeet and Trap Championship and an awards ceremony that was held after the May 17, 1992 board meeting. Keeping in tune with a safety mindset, in May of 1992, donations were accepted by Dr. Thomas Breza to purchase a defibrillator and professional oxygen tank. The total needed for the purchase was $7000. Additionally, in June, the lodge was designated as a smoke-free area.

In July of 1992, hunt committee member, Lew Whiting, taught a class on how to make plaster casts of animal footprints as part of the animal tracking program planned for Labor Day weekend of that year. The casts then became part of the craft show also planned for that weekend. The craft event was titled "Show and Tell". The hunt committee donated a large BBQ grill to the Birds Nest, and donated and built the BBQ gazebo shelter in August of 1992.

BBQ and gazebo at Birds Nest

Then on August 15, the "SOLD OUT" celebration was held at the lodge. This well-attended and joyous event, hosted by Hammock Associates, Inc., celebrated the sale of the final lot. This was arguably one of the highest attended celebrations that Indian Hammock had ever seen.

After the recent vandalism to the Hammock amenities and the burglary of a home, the board unanimously approved a motion to request that the Okeechobee County Sheriff's Office increase their routine patrols through the Indian Hammock property.

Besides vandalism and burglary, poachers were a big problem for the community. At the next month's board meeting, a motion was approved to invite the game warden to Indian Hammock to review the poaching situation.

Florida Statute 720 governing homeowner associations was voted into law and effective October 1, 1992. One aspect of the new law required changes in the board of directors election process. The Election Committee Chair, Joan Powell, made the required changes. The new process was approved at the October 1992 board meeting in preparation for the January members meeting and election.

CHAPTER 5
Working Through the Growing Pains

Nearly twenty years had passed since Al Cone's dream first took root and, at the January 1993 members meeting, the membership was given a summary of the 2 decades of progress. Some of the highlights included: 22 structures and 15 vehicles owned, 12 miles of shell rock road, 18 miles of grass roads, 93 homes built or under construction and 33 full-time families (including 2 resident employees).

In March of 1993, the Management Committee was directed by the board to appoint a special committee to come up with a proposal for a paid manager. By the next meeting in April, the board approved the committee's recommendation to appoint Indian Hammock and board of director member, Jim Lassiter, as the full-time manager for a salary of $20,000 per year. His employment took effect immediately. Also approved around the same time was the hiring of an administrative assistant. Filling the position was Tammy Potter.

The newly appointed property manager, who worked closely with the management committee and the board, now handled day-to-day operations.

In July of 1993, the board accepted the proposal for a new electronic gate at a proposed cost of $11,168.26. The gate was operated by remote control transmitters, much like a garage door opener, that were issued to members for a $30.00 refundable deposit. The project was funded by members' donations of $6500, Hunt Committee donations of $4000, and the balance paid from the Indian Hammock budget.

At the end of the manager's first year of employment, a committee was formed to complete his performance evaluation. At the May 1994 board meeting, the committee chair, George Arata, reported that Mr. Lassiter had met and exceeded all expectations of the management position. Specific accomplishments mentioned were: writing job descriptions for all of the employees, setting up a chain of command, and decreasing the club's debt while increasing its cash position. This glowing evaluation brought forth a motion by the board that his annual salary be increased from $20,000 to $30,000 effective May 1, 1994. The motion passed unanimously.

In June, the board of directors established the first standing Finance Committee and established the club treasurer as the standing committee chair.

Also at the June 1994 meeting, the board established a committee to build an exercise room (now referred to as the fitness center). At the August board meeting, Fitness Committee Chair, Bill Black, reported that the plans for the fitness center were near completion. By October, fund-raisers were underway to collect the $12,000 needed to purchase the building supplies. The labor was all donated by members, as was the exercise equipment to fill the room.

Administrative assistant, Tammy Potter, tendered her resignation and was replaced on November 22, 1994 by Cheryl Speight.

At the January 1995 board meeting, newly elected president, Bill Dover, spoke of the uniqueness of Indian Hammock and suggested that to ensure Indian Hammock's long term success, his objective for 1995 would be to "re-establish the small town atmosphere. An atmosphere where residents anticipated the needs of their neighbors and community and rallied to those needs by working together for the good of the community".

Action at the January 1995 meeting included accepting the Cow Pasture Committee's recommendation to enter into a lease with Mr. Fulford and Mr. Goolsby at $6,000 per year with a lease term of five years.

Additionally, a motion was passed to purchase the required USPS mailboxes and submit a request for individually sorted mail. The post office was contacted and Indian Hammock was advised that in order for mail to be sorted and delivered to each mailbox, each lot must have a mailbox. The mailboxes were then ordered at a total cost of $5,628. The construction plans for the building to house the mailboxes was approved at the May 1995 meeting.

In May of 1995, a beautification project hosted by the Recreation Committee began at the Foster Recreation Area and around Foster Lake. Eleven sabal palms, nine of which were donated by members, were planted and lovingly watered by volunteers.

Palm trees donated by members

Over the remaining months of the year, other members also donated trees to the area, including several oak trees.

The construction of the building covering the mailboxes was completed over the summer of 1995 and in August the mailboxes were delivered and installed. Then finally, after five years of waiting, sorted mail service began on September 25.

Also over the summer, the Exercise and Fitness Committee collected donated items and conducted a fundraising auction. The auction proceeds were $17,738. By the end of the year, the total donations received were $21,534. Due to the success of the fund-raising efforts, the committee proposed seeking bids from a contractor to complete the bulk of the construction. The volunteers would then complete the finishing work. The board approved this plan and over the next several months, the committee began the work of requesting and reviewing bids.

In November 1995, property manager, Jim Lassiter, announced his pending retirement effective March 1, allowing time for him to orient the new manager. At the board meeting that month, a search committee was appointed. The committee members were: Jim Lassiter, Gene Brioschi, Wes Holder, Julie Huebner, Lew Whiting, Ed Foster, George Arata, Paula Sarvis, and Walter Jolly.

The committee prepared a job description for the position and began conducting interviews with the applicants in January 1996. The management committee was instructed to make the final decision on who would be hired as long as the vote of the committee was unanimous; otherwise, the selection was to be brought to the board. At the February 1996 meeting, the manager's report was given by the new manager (still in training), John Lynch.

In March of 1996, Maria Wolf requested that a plot of land 120 ft. by 120 ft. adjacent to the lodge entrance road be designated for a lawn bowling green. The board approved the concept, but did not give full approval to the project until the committee was able to provide more information regarding the cost factors related to establishing and maintaining the green. This information was to be submitted to the Recreation Committee for coordination and final acceptance by the Management Committee.

The Hammock was hit with very sad news on April 28, 1996 when they were notified that Ed Foster had passed away at his Indian Hammock home at the age of 77. In honor of this devoted friend of Indian Hammock, the board unanimously passed a motion that his seat on the board would remain vacant for the rest of 1996.

The sign designating the location of the Edward T. Foster Recreation Area was completed and hung in early September of 1996. Then on September 15, immediately after the board meeting, a memorial service was held at the recreation area. This well-attended memorial gave the members of Indian Hammock a chance to share their fond memories of Ed and honor his commitment to the community.

Edward T. Foster Recreation Area sign

In December of 1996, the planning was completed for the Fitness Center and the contract was awarded to Conkling Construction, owned by member Don Conkling. The final contracted price was $28,679 with community donations covering all but $7,000. At the same meeting, the board agreed to pay the shortfall out of the budget. By March of 1997, the building was completed, except for painting to be completed by the volunteers. Once the volunteers put the finishing touches on the building, the members could join for an annual cost of $25.00. To finish the project, rules and regulations were completed and a grand opening was scheduled.

The Inaugural Ed Foster Memorial Fun Shoot was held in February 1997 at the skeet and trap field. The winner of the shoot was Lew Whiting. The Class-A winner was Al Weidenfeller and the Class-B winner was Don Conkling. A painting by Robert Butler of a panther stalking turkeys was donated to the Skeet and Trap Committee by the Foster family as a memorial trophy for the annual shoot. The painting was hung in the dining room of the lodge and the winner's name was added to a plaque that accompanied the trophy.

Robert Butler painting of panther

At the April board meeting, Maria Wolf gave an update on the progress of the fund-raising for the construction of the lawn bowling green and the proposed maintenance expenses.

Indian Hammock's first employee, Roger Brewer, completed 20 years of service with Indian Hammock on May 25, 1997. At the May board meeting, a resolution was read and recorded in the minutes formally congratulating him and "wishing him continued success in his service to the corporation and its members". Along with the resolution, President John Hume presented Roger with a buck knife.

Roger Brewer

In November of 1997, early construction of the lawn bowling green began. The expenses were covered by the committee's fund-raisers and by many volunteers donating their time to assist with the construction.

By the end of 1997, John Lynch reported that 250 members owned 299 lots. There were 116 homes built and 4 under construction. Sixty of the homes were primary residences.

At the January 18, 1998 board meeting, a motion was made and unanimously approved to separate the food service function of the lodge from the social functions. The food service management was assigned to the manager and the Management Committee and the new Special Events Committee handled the social functions for the community. The Lodge Committee was disbanded.

In February of 1998, the Equestrian Committee teamed with the Jupiter Horseman's Association to host a 25-mile ride throughout the Hammock. The committee also announced the planned move of the pony pasture from the east side of Gator Cave to the west side. This area was larger and would allow for more pony boarding. They also planned new stalls and fencing for the pasture. The previous pony pasture was then designated as an isolation area. Also that month, the committee coordinated with the Remuda Club and provided the club with a separate pasture for their horses. A portion of the pasture east of the arena was chosen for the Remuda Club horses.

Major work on amenities was the order of business for March and April of 1998, when the cabana was renovated and the tennis courts resurfaced. The total cost of both projects was just under thirty thousand dollars, paid by either the budget or reserve funds.

By May of 1998, the trailer near the gate was no longer used as housing for Indian Hammock employees. Manager, John Lynch, worked with the county sheriff to arrange for a resident deputy to take over the trailer. As with most courtesy officers, the housing was offered rent-free in exchange for patrols of the community. Once the agreement was worked out, the trailer was given a facelift
that included an interior renovation and the placement of a roof-over system. Upon completion, Deputy Sheriff Greg McDevitt and his K9 partner moved in on June 1, 1998 becoming Indian Hammock's first resident deputy.

On May 15, for the first time, the community enjoyed a dinner and theater night at the lodge as a fund-raising event for the Lawn Bowling Committee. After a spaghetti dinner, 24 members had an opportunity to exercise their thespian skills in a Lawn Bowling Committee original production.

I spoke to Karey Brown about the evening of the play and the laughs everyone enjoyed. She explained that the script, written by member Janis Pond, was titled, "The Call of the Wild" and sub-titled, "The 24th Annual Meeting of the Indian Hammock Wildlife". This musical comedy was a parody of a board meeting as it would be conducted by some of the Indian Hammock wildlife. She saved many pictures from the play, the original script, song lyrics, and the program (see photo). The cast included: Billy Bobcat played by Corey Miller, Shirley Fox played by Karen Sands, John Deer played by Ana Ciorrocco, Deputy Armadillo played by Fifi Lynch, Davie Squirrel played by Wes Holder, and Rick Coon played by John Pond. The original production program listed the remaining supporting cast and production crew members.

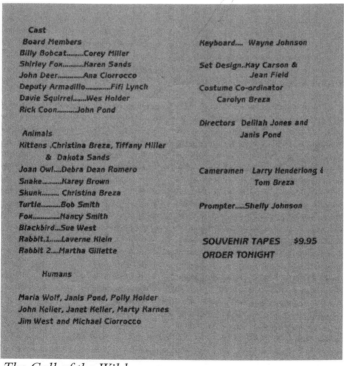

The Call of the Wild program

From the moment the "curtain" rose, until the final bow, the audience was treated to top-notch entertainment and nonstop comedy, all in support of the Lawn Bowling Committee. The original songs were titled: "As Man Moves in Here" to the tune of "When Johnny Comes Marching Home", "Docs" to the tune of "When the Saints Go Marching In", and "Pet Song" to the tune of "Old McDonald Had a Farm". The final song was "I'd Like to Teach the World to Sing", made famous in a Coca-Cola commercial in the 1970's. At the conclusion of the final song, Billy Bobcat called for the "meeting" to adjourn. The motion was seconded by Davie Squirrel and passed unanimously with the usual all-in-favor howl. After the final curtain, the cast and crew performed one final cheer. The cheer went like this, "Indian Hammock, we love you. Wildlife and humans too! Fun we poke, that's an act. We love you, that's a fact. Yeah Hammock!!"

In the summer of 1998, the Okeechobee County Commission adopted a new ordinance, effective on October 1, mandating residential garbage collection, with an annual fee of $108.56 per residential unit. After the Indian Hammock Board's discussion with Commissioner Hazellief, the ordinance was revised at the next commission meeting. At Commissioner Hazellief's urging, the ordinance was revised so that private homeowner associations, such as Indian Hammock, would be considered commercial; thereby, exempt from the annual residential lot fee.

In the fall of 1998, the board was notified of the planned widening and resurfacing of US 441 in front of the property. The plan called for adding four feet of roadway to each side of 441. The board asked member, Barbara Roberts, to contact the Florida Department of Transportation and request the addition of a turn lane into Indian Hammock. Unfortunately, after the traffic patterns were studied, it was determined that the State of Florida would not fund such a project. However, FDOT stated that Indian Hammock could fund the turn lane at a cost of $30,000. Barbara recommended that all of the members contact the FDOT traffic operations manager and our state representative via phone calls and letters to elicit their support. Unfortunately, even with the calls and letters, the FDOT did not change their decision.

At the November 15, 1998 board meeting, the first Membership Committee was established. This new and ongoing committee was to have at least three members who would be responsible for obtaining and reviewing backgrounds and credit checks. The first committee members were Ken Finney, Ray Jones, Wes Holder, and Chica Stracener. Consideration was given to imposing a $100 application fee that would cover the cost of the screening and lunch during the new member orientation.

The beginning of 1999 brought news that the much used and loved wooden deck around the lodge had rotted beyond repair and would need to be replaced or removed. The board charged the manager with the task of obtaining estimates for a replacement wooden deck. Bids were also solicited for a concrete deck. In May, while still in the bidding stage, the deck was removed completely and temporary stairs were built at the emergency exits. At the June 1999 meeting, the bids for a wooden deck were presented. The larger deck design initially approved carried a price tag of $16,000-$17,000 and the proposed alternate smaller wraparound deck came in at $10,000. No bids were presented for a concrete deck. Since no further mention of replacing the deck was found in all of the minutes, I contacted John Lynch and asked him about the project. John explained that a decision was never made after the cost estimates were presented, and the project "basically died after that".

Acoustics in the dining room of the lodge had been an ongoing issue, with the manager actively seeking a solution. After several recommendations, it was decided to purchase and install sound absorbing draperies throughout the room.

Also in May, Fred and LaVerne Klein were appointed as webmasters for Indian Hammock's first website. The website was setup to be a supplement to the Hammock Herald and included committee news, pictures, and classified ads. Although the website did not have a dedicated domain name, it could be easily accessed by going to http://www.cris.com/~mgklein/ih/ index/shtml.

Additionally, in May, Marilyn Kluegel began her employment as secretary/administrative assistant. One of her first accomplishments was to setup a computer program for inventory control. This program greatly improved efficiency and accuracy of the operation.

Prior to June of 1999, the membership was excluded from participating in the cattle pasture lease. At the June meeting, the board unanimously voted to allow both members and outsiders to bid for the lease. The new cattle lease was awarded to Miller/Hickman in August of 1999 to commence on March 1, 2000. The term was 10 years with an annual rate of $9,000 per year for the first five years and $12,000 per year for the final five years.

Effective September 20, 1999 the area code for Indian Hammock was changed from 941 to its current 863.

A quorum was not achieved for the October board meeting due to Hurricane Irene. The four members who braved the heavy rains and gusty winds were Corey Miller, Chica Stracener, Charlie Whipple, and Lew Whiting.

The new millennium was ushered in by the first Single Action Cowboy shoot at the rifle/pistol range on January 15, 2000. The fun event was followed by a tailgate party. All of the attendees wore their finest cowboy and cowgirl attire and embraced their new nicknames. Winners of the men's pistol division were "Ike", "Redneck", and "Dusty" who were known off the range as Scott Behrens, Gus Roberts, and Ken Finney. The women's winners were "Little Stormy", "Plinker Belle", and "Hothead" who were also known as LaVerne Klein, Janice Whiting, and Heather Finney. The men's long rifle winners were "Blind Bart" and "Shaky Slim", whose off the range names were Gary Neff and Larry Pendleton.

The fun times continued and lodge meal attendance doubled, with credit given to Special Events Chair, Diane Pendleton, who planned wonderful monthly parties.
By the beginning of 2000, the total number of homes had risen to 130 with six more under construction. Although the membership enjoyed the progress, it came with a new set of troubles. The increased use of the roads by the many new residents and the construction vehicles had taken a toll on the main roads. It was apparent to all that substantial work was needed. The Management Committee, in conjunction with the newly formed Road Review Committee, recommended applying a layer of shell rock over the existing road from the gate to the stables and from the flagpole around to Big Buck Slough (near the road that leads to the burn pile). However,

the funds for such a large project were well beyond what were in the annual road maintenance budget.

In February 2000, a special assessment was levied for repair of the roads as recommended by both the road review and management committees. Each lot was assessed $600 to cover the cost of applying the 6 inches of shell rock that was needed. Work was scheduled to start no later than April 3, 2000.

Pool resurfacing work began on February 21, 2000. Once the work was completed, Gail MacLain, as part of the Exercise and Fitness Committee, conducted the first AquaAerobics class in May 2000. Ongoing classes, open to both men and women, continued three times per week with morning and evening classes.

By the April board meeting, 245 lots had paid their special assessments. It was at that meeting that the board unanimously voted to handle the delinquent accounts as follows: impose a finance charge 1½% per month (18% per year) on all outstanding balances, impose loss of privileges to use the amenities on accounts 60 days late, and direct the club attorney to file liens against accounts over 90 days delinquent. An additional legal fee charge of $150 was billed to each member's account if submitted for lien.

By July 2000, the work on the roads was completed and the new sod along the shoulders had taken root. With the roads improved, the Management Committee recommended increasing the speed limit from 20 mph to 25 mph, except that it would remain 10 mph near the stables. The board approved the recommendation and approved the allocation of $350 to replace the speed limit signs.

Even with the new layer of shell rock applied, the dust from traffic continued. The Road Review Committee now turned their attention to dust suppression and sought viable and cost effective options. When their research was completed, they recommended the test application of a road bind material. Before purchasing the product, the committee recommended using it on a test area. The area chosen was the first 1/3 of a mile from the gate toward the flagpole. Natural Solutions Corporation furnished the material known as Roadbind Ultra Plus to cover the test area at no charge. The community was hopeful that road bind would be the solution to the dust issue, but they also knew that only "time would tell if this was the solution".

As in the previous years, safety of the members was a high priority. In August of 2000, the board approved soliciting donations to offset the $3630 cost of purchasing the first automatic external defibrillator (AED). By the following month, all of the funds were collected to proceed with the equipment purchase. The Fitness Committee donated $1000 from committee funds, and other members donated an additional $1370. The balance was paid from the Indian Hammock budget. The Management Committee recommended that the AED be kept at the office, since it was the most centralized location. Members and staff were required to be both AED and CPR certified to use the AED. Member, Dee Patton, a Nurse Practitioner and Certified CPR Instructor, donated her time giving free CPR classes, with the first class held on October 7, 2000.

The 2000 Labor Day weekend festivities included a Sock Hop Drive-In Dinner Party held at the lodge, with music provided by Jerry and the Hurricanes. Also held that weekend was a

Rubber Ducky Race in the pool to benefit the Lawn Bowling Committee. Rubber ducks were available to purchase for $8 or two for $15. The water aquatic group provided the wave action and judging of the winning ducks. A total of 144 ducks were purchased for the race and prizes were awarded for first, second, and third place.

At the September 2000 board meeting, Lew Whiting advised everyone that, over the past several months, there were several instances of irresponsibility and dangerous usage of the range facility. Specific incidents mentioned at the meeting were a round was shot through the east storage closet in the direction of the horse pasture and houses, and a shotgun was fired through the roof of the range shelter. Lew recommended to the board that a Rifle & Pistol Range Committee be established. Also submitted were the proposed list of rules, hours of operation, qualification requirements, and fines to be imposed for violations. The committee was approved by the board and the new rules went into effect on November 1st after the membership was notified in the October Hammock Herald.

The holiday season kicked off with the annual Christmas parade held on November 25 with approximately 100 people in attendance. Santa, played by John Vernalia, was a big hit with the children when he arrived to take his seat in his F150 "sleigh". Then on December 9, four members (Finney, Behrens, Stevens, and Stracener) opened their festively-decorated homes for the annual Tour of Homes hosted by the Lawn Bowling Committee. Finally, on December 16, the annual Christmas dinner was held at the lodge, followed by candlelight caroling.

The spring of 2001 was a difficult time with two brush fires and a break-in at the lodge. The first fire started on March 20 at 1:30 in the afternoon on lot 40. The ample spring winds of 15-20 mph quickly sent the fire over Hawks View North, surging north and eastward, quickly jumping the north fence line. By 11 pm, fire crews from the Division of Forestry, Okeechobee Fire Rescue, and volunteers from the Fort Drum, Buckhead Ridge, Bassinger, and Lorida fire departments finally contained the fire. By the next morning, the damaged was assessed at over 100 acres burned, but no homes in Indian Hammock were lost. Our north fence line neighbor, Rocking K Ranch, did not fare as well though, losing his mobile home in the blaze.

The smoke had barely settled from the March 20 fire when the second wildfire started on April 25 behind lots 211 and 212 along Boggie Branch. A much smaller area was burned in this fire thanks to the First Responder volunteers of Indian Hammock and the Division of Forestry, who extinguished the flames quickly with the use of foaming agent injected into the water.

A group of teens having a party at the pool on June 7, 2001 threw the furniture into the pool and left broken glass around the deck. Then, part of the group wandered over to the lodge where they caused more damage. Besides ripping five screens, the group broke into the kitchen where they stole food and then used the lodge appliances to cook the raw items. After being caught red-handed by a Hammock employee, the teens were charged by the Okeechobee Sheriff's Office with trespassing, breaking and entering, and criminal mischief. Although an apology letter was received and partial restitution was made to Indian Hammock, the board voted unanimously to press charges against all of the youths involved.

At the July 2001 board meeting, the lawn bowling area was officially named the "Maria Wolf Lawn Bowling Green" to honor the many years of hard work and dedication that made her dream come true.

By October of 2001, core samples were taken of the test area of Indian Hammock Trail to determine the effectiveness of the road bind material. In addition to substantial dust suppression, the treated area testing indicated no loss of shell rock; whereas, the core samples from the untreated roads showed a surface loss of ½" to 1½".

John Lynch presented the costs to complete the road bind project on approximate 4.5 miles of the main roads and for follow-up maintenance. The vendor initially told John Lynch that the total cost for the initial application was $59,500, with a rejuvenation needed in 6 months at a cost of $10,500. Thereafter, annual rejuvenations were required at the same price. The board voted 4 to 6, defeating the motion to proceed with the road bind material.

I spoke to John Lynch about the road bind project and about why it had failed to get the board's support. John explained that two problems were discovered after the manufacturer provided the initial quote. The first problem was that the reapplications needed to be much more frequent than initially stated, thereby increasing the cost estimates significantly. The second problem involved how the treated road surface responded to even the lightest rain. Rain caused the top portion of the road surface to become slushy, as it typically does; however, the treated road slush that splashed onto the car's body and into the wheel wells adhered and hardened like concrete.

At the annual members meeting in January 2002, it was reported that 9 new homes had been completed with 4 more under construction. That brought the total number of homes to 139. Of these, 88 were occupied by year-round residents, an increase of 22 from the previous year.

On March 2, 2002, Indian Hammock suffered its worst wildfire in 6 years. A campfire, thought to have been extinguished, was left unattended by the owners of lot 255. Winds upwards of 20 mph fanned the smoldering fire, blowing embers outside of the containment area and igniting what was ultimately a 230-acre fire. By what was referred to as a miracle, fifteen homes in the path of the raging wildfire were spared and there was no loss of human life. Fire crews responded from Okeechobee County Fire Rescue, Division of Forestry, and volunteers from Ft. Drum, Lorida, Buckhead Ridge, and Kenansville. Indian Hammock residents who were not helping fight the fire helped in other ways, including providing food and drinks to the fire crews. Additionally, County Commissioner, David Hazellief, brought food donated by the Okeechobee Publix to the fire scene. Residents continued to fight hot spot flare-ups for the next several weeks.

2002 forest fire damage

In April, the Division of Forestry advised the board that it was imperative that the burnt trees be removed as soon as possible before pine beetle infestation. Forestry provided the names of several reputable timber removal companies and the information was passed on to the lot owners affected by the fire.

In April of 2002, John Lynch requested and was awarded by the board the sum of $2500 to purchase five sets of firefighting bunker gear. The new equipment was kept in duffle bags on the trucks to be available for use by anyone assisting with firefighting duties.

The landscape remained dotted with burnt pine tree stumps until April 29 when Atlantic Timber was finally able to mobilize crews to harvest all available dead trees. The unsightly timber was removed from lots 239-254, as well as some of the common land in the area of lots 238 and 239. The project was finally completed on May 11.

At the May board meeting, first Indian Hammock employee, Roger Brewer, was recognized for achieving the milestone of being a 25-year employee as of May 24, 2002. A letter of thanks and congratulations was read and presented to him.

In the summer of 2002, the entry gate was converted from a remote-control entry system to a card-swipe system. The access cards were programmed to identify the assigned user with each swipe.

In January of 2003, a committee was established to determine the number and size of trees needed within the 40-acres of common land to replace those destroyed in the March fire. To move toward a settlement, the committee was to contact the owner of lot 255 to obtain the claim number and adjuster's name. The committee members were John Lynch, Barbara Pearl, Mitchell Walker, and Chair Ken Finney.

In February, the board was notified that according to Florida Statute 712, and specifically the Florida Marketable Record Titles Act, a homeowner association's covenants and restrictions may be rendered unenforceable and extinguished after 30 years if not properly reaffirmed by the association beforehand. Indian Hammock's documents were recorded on November 2, 1973. In order to keep Indian Hammock's Declaration of Restrictions in force, a special members meeting was scheduled for July 20, 2003. Stephanie Pearson was designated to coordinate and oversee the voting.

In April 2003, the Dust Suppression Committee was established to study ways to mitigate the dust from the roads by means other than asphalt. The committee members were Ken Finney, Barbara Roberts, Ray Jones, Dee Patton, Dr. Wayne Johnson, and Chair Maureen Kleiman.

On July 20, 2003, the special meeting of the membership was held. Acting Chairman of Elections, Stephanie Pearson, advised that a quorum was achieved with 32 voters present holding a combined total of 129 proxies. The vote count ended with 154 for and 7 against the renewal of the Declarations of Restrictions for 30 years. The updated documents were then recorded with Okeechobee County.

In September 2003, eighteen months after the March 2002 wildfire, the insurance claim was settled. After mediation, Indian Hammock received $23,000 for damage to the common grounds.

The Road Dust Suppression Committee completed its exhaustive investigation and at the October board meeting recommended the application of the product, Ultra Bond 2000, used in the Villages of Wellington. They further recommended applying the product to a ½-mile test area at a cost of $4,746.60. This price included professional application and training of the Hammock staff on the ongoing day-to-day maintenance. The board accepted the committee's recommendation, but voted unanimously to apply the product to a 1.4-mile test area at a cost of $8,213.50.

At the conclusion of a safety survey by the risk management department of our insurance company, it was recommended that the pool be fenced. John Lynch presented bids for 3 different types of fencing at the December 2003 meeting. The board voted unanimously to accept the bid for a green vinyl fence at a cost of $3077.

A huge crowd of 128 members dressed in their "denims & black ties" celebrated at the annual members party on January 17, 2004. After dining on roast prime rib of beef, Caesar salad, and baked potato, they danced the night away to the music of DJ, Jumpin' Junior.

The first Indian Hammock website was retired in February 2004. Special thanks was given to Fred and LaVerne Klein for their four and a half years of service updating the website on a monthly basis.

The members of the Remuda Club continued to enjoy riding on the five club horses, including two recently acquired mares, Lexus and Maria. Steve Rubin was thanked by the club for his guidance in selecting both horses and for his ongoing help and knowledge.

A dry spring in 2004 was at least partially to blame for fires of unknown origin on May 27 and May 29. The first was near lot 272, but was quickly extinguished by neighbors and first responders. Unfortunately, the second was larger, involving three lots and several acres of common land. Due to the quick response of the Okeechobee County Fire Department and the Division of Forestry, there was no damage to anyone's home.

With the dry spring, the application of the dust suppressant became even more necessary. Unfortunately, the company that provided the dust suppressant, Ultra Bond 2000, went out of business. However, after several telephone contacts, John Lynch was able to find the same solution through B&B Oil of Georgia. Their product was known as Coherex.

The Indian Hammock maintenance crew was able to equip the Hammock's 2600-gallon water tank trailer with a pressure pump and spray bar to facilitate applications of the Coherex.

CHAPTER 6
Fury Unleashed Brings Us Together

Indian Hammock was visited by 3 unwelcome guests in the summer of 2004. The first, Hurricane Charley, blew into town on August 19, 2004. Although Charley was much tougher on some of the towns to our west, he ushered in relief to the dry conditions. By the morning of the 20th, the damage was assessed as minor with only the loss of power and several downed trees. The Indian Hammock maintenance crew was quick to respond and within 2 days it was business as usual.

However, the peace was to be short-lived. On August 21, a weather system, that we would come to know as Frances, developed off the west coast of Africa. Frances meandered across the Atlantic picking up speed and strength on her way. Just after midnight on September 5, Frances made landfall almost directly over Stuart with sustained winds of 100 mph. That morning, her eye passed directly over Lake Okeechobee.

By September 6, the severe weather had moved out of the Hammock and the members assessed the damage. John Lynch provided the board with a facilities damage report at the September board meeting. John's damage report included: the horse hospital that was damaged beyond repair, a large section of the arena fencing was destroyed, a canopy and section of roof on the old barn was seriously damaged, and the roof of the Remuda Club horse stalls was damaged. Other buildings lost some shingles and more trees were lost, including some large oak trees. At the airstrip, the most severe damage was to the 5-bay hanger that had its doors ripped off. Some of the planes suffered damage as well.

The insurance adjusters were still calculating the losses when the name Jeanne was first uttered.

With damages from Charley and Frances still fresh in the members' minds, all attention was suddenly turned to tracking another hurricane. Her name was Jeanne, but she was no lady. As she chugged across the Atlantic, Jeanne strengthened, becoming a major hurricane on September 25. Early on the morning of the 26th, the center of Jeanne's 60-mile-wide eye made landfall on the Florida coast near Stuart, at virtually the identical spot that Frances had come ashore three weeks earlier. Maximum winds at the time of landfall were estimated to be near 120 mph. Although she had lost some wind strength before her eye made a direct hit on the Hammock, the estimated sustained winds were still 80 mph with gusts to 120 mph. Additionally, as typically happens in hurricanes, Jeanne spawned many tornados.

The saturated Hammock could do nothing but hunker down and ride it out. Only memories remained of the recent dry spring, as members watched the already wet ground give way to widespread flooding. By the end of the day, Jeanne had moved out of the Hammock weakening to a tropical storm over Tampa before turning north.

With his humor still intact, John Lynch started his October 22 manager's report by saying, "This is like watching the sequel to a bad B movie". However, his full report was not something to laugh at. John shared that many homes were damaged and nearly every power line on the property was downed. Almost every roadway and driveway was blocked by fallen trees or flooding, affecting approximately 20 of the 26 miles of roadways.

Although property was damaged, the members became a bright spot in the post-disaster clean-up. Neighbors reached out to one another, putting aside any former disputes as they worked side-by-side rebuilding what Jeanne tried to take away.

John Lynch hired two contractors to assist with the recovery. Besides clearing trees, the contractors removed debris at the 5-bay hanger that was now a total loss. Nearly every club building suffered damage to some degree.

Hurricane damage to a hangar

Hurricane damage to a skeet house

In November, the Architectural Review Committee was very busy reviewing and approving members' plans for six new roofs and one water shed. The committee remained busy in December when five additional new roofs were approved. Although the committee's work slowed by January 2005, they did approve replacement of three more hurricane-damaged roofs.

The rebuilding continued into 2005 with committees contributing labor to rebuild their amenities. Work teams from the Equestrian and Stable Committee conducted a fence building party to help defray the cost of rebuilding the arena fencing. The total savings to Indian Hammock was $5000. The Skeet and Trap Committee also donated their time to reconstruction of the damaged skeet house.

Possibly prompted by the three major hurricanes of 2004, the first "Clean-up the Hammock Day" was held on February 12. Families, including children and grandchildren, gathered at the stables to receive trash bags to fill. After hours of clean-up, all of the helpers enjoyed a complimentary lunch at the Birds Nest.

By March, life around the Hammock gradually returned to normal. With the work crews no longer needed for the post-hurricane repairs, it was finally time for the members to begin enjoying fun times together again. One of those times was the Eat 'n Fly hosted by the pilots. A nice crowd of 87 arrived for a quick flight around the Hammock followed by a lunch. The pilots who gave of their time and talents were: Jack Shahan, Joe Ragon, Dotty Westby, Jerry Farquhar, and Monte Pollock. Ground crew helpers were Dave Minor, Roger Caldwell, and Kyle Jansen.

By April of 2005, the 2004 hurricanes were becoming a distant, painful memory. However, the full impact of the financial burden of the recovery was still very much on everyone's mind. The emergency reserve fund of $250,000 had been reduced to a meager $80,000 and the new 2005 hurricane season was beginning in just over one month. The board voted to impose a $60 per lot/per month special assessment until the reserve returned to $250,000 (anticipated to be about 10 months).

However, nature did not wait. April brought more winds to the Hammock, this time in the form of a tornado. On Saturday morning, April 2, a tornado whipped through the pasture areas and office/maintenance barn complex ultimately causing over $65,000 in damage. As they did after the hurricanes, the members mobilized to assist in the recovery. The tornado had demolished the paddock fencing and stripped away half of the office/maintenance barn roof. Volunteers placed tarps over the open roof areas and covered the office furniture and equipment with Visqueen.

By July, the insurance claim had been settled and rebuilding of the office complex began. Besides a new roof, the office received new flooring, A/C duct system, A/C air handler, mold remediation, and fresh paint. During the repairs, the office operations were relocated temporarily to the recently vacated bunkhouse.

In July 2005, the board approved the purchase of a pool heater to make year-round swimming comfortable. The water fitness group, Indian Hammock Seahorses, and the Quilting Group got busy planning fund-raisers to cover the cost of the electric bill for the heater. The first event was an arts and crafts show held on September 4. Thanks to the vendors, volunteers, and buyers, the proceeds totaled $2,270.

By October, the repairs to the office/ maintenance complex were nearly completed, and office operations were still conducted in the bunkhouse. Then, like a never-ending story, the Hammock began tracking yet another hurricane. This time her name was Wilma. Although Indian Hammock was spared a direct hit, the nearly-completed new roof at the office was torn off. Once again, the landscape was dotted with downed and broken pine trees. The office operations finally returned home when the building repairs were completed in mid-January 2006.

The 10th Annual Ed Foster Memorial Shoot was held at the skeet and trap field on Sunday, February 5. The winners were Lew Whiting, Al Weidenfeller, and George Arata.

Also in February, the Rifle/Pistol Range was closed for remodeling and a Range Remodeling Committee was formed. Members on the committee were Lew Whiting, Bob Huebner, and Walt Hornberger. The committee later added members Jon Newman and Rich Hogue.

The board signed an agreement with the NRA to send out a representative from their Range Department to evaluate the range facility and provide the committee with recommendations for remodeling. Member, Lew Whiting, personally paid the $400 that was charged for the service. The NRA evaluation was completed and the plans were presented at the April board meeting. The newly renovated complex was to be setup with three different ranges, consisting of a handgun range of 25 yards, a small-bore range of 50 yards, and a high-power range of 100 yards. The report called for enlarging and redesigning the dirt berms at the facility, creating new administrative guidelines for the facility, and establishing a NRA certified Range Safety Officer program.

With the plan ready and board approved, the committee started a fund-raising campaign. Construction began a short time later and the new range SOP was approved at the July board meeting. The NRA required that the Range Safety Officer class be taught by NRA certified Chief Range Safety Officers. The Hammock could pay the NRA to send its instructors, or some members could attend the Instructor/CRSO training and become certified to teach it. Lew and Janice Whiting obtained CRSO certification and conducted the first RSO class on August 25, 2006. Classes were held monthly for several months to accommodate the interested shooters. Finally, on September 17, the newly renovated range was reopened to many happy shooters.

During the spring of 2006, the topic of road dust was again on the minds of the members. Unfortunately, the Coherex that was thought to be the answer to the dusty roads was not successful. I spoke to John Lynch to get more details as to why it had failed. John explained that not only was the cost per reapplication considerably higher than initially quoted, but also the need for reapplications was more frequent than initially estimated. The board decided to suspend any further applications of Coherex and directed the Management Committee to seek other viable options to control the dust.

The committee researched several options before seeking more information on a product called Chip Seal. The committee even went to another community to see the product in use. After several meetings, the Management Committee reported their findings at the August 2006 board meeting. The cost of the applying Chip Seal from the gate to the flagpole was quoted as $66,065, and from the gate to the stables and from the flagpole around to Big Buck was $265,093. The cost to cover all of the main roads was $421,471. The Chip Seal was estimated to last 10 years before reapplication was needed. No vote was taken to move forward with the road surface; however, the vote to poll the membership to obtain their feelings about the use of the product passed. Over the next 2 months, members voiced their concern about the product, citing the long-term costs, potential for speeding to increase, and objections to a special assessment. No vote was ever taken by the members or board, so the topic died.

In February 2007, thanks to the hard work of Manager John Lynch, Indian Hammock was granted the designation of a "Firewise Community" by the Division of Forestry.

According to this program's Firewise Mitigation Plan, a Firewise community's first priority for fire protection is to reduce the vegetative fuel within the residential areas. The board established a Firewise Committee and its first members were Barbara Roberts, Kyle Jansen, and Doug Watler. (Both Kyle and Doug work as full-time firefighters.)

In February 2007, a group of 25 volunteers completed a study to determine the number of and variety of birds that call Indian Hammock home. The count included both full-time dwellers and snow birds (the feathered type, not our human friends from the north). The group counted over 2000 birds of 70 different species.

As the study took the volunteers into the wooded areas of the Hammock, they also encountered many other animals, including raccoons, grey squirrels, deer, otters, field mice, alligators, and fox squirrels.

In the spring of 2007, the resident deputy's mobile home was deemed no longer safe for human occupancy. John Lynch reported that a replacement mobile home would cost $69,000. The board voted unanimously to take the necessary steps to remove the mobile home. No alternative housing was approved and the resident deputy program was suspended.

There were whispers all around the Hammock during June and right up to July 7th when the membership held a surprise party celebrating Maria Wolf's 95th birthday. After the candles were blown out, the light show continued over at the airstrip where "George Arata & company" hosted the Independence Day fireworks display.

In September of 2007, exiting Indian Hammock became a little safer. Due to the hard work and many business connections of Bob Huebner, the DOT instituted the "no passing zone" on U.S. Hwy 441 at 328th Trail, with the appropriate road markings.

By October, fall was in the air, the weather was not much cooler, but something new and fun was about to be introduced. The Community Service Committee requested and received approval to host the first Trunk or Treat/ Fall Festival. The empty field across from the stables was soon transformed into a wonderful fall scene. Corn stalks, hay bales, and pumpkins filled the field, as did game booths and a trailer converted into a country-style bandstand.

Then on October 27, the festively decorated "trunks" arrived. Soon the field was filled with giggling, costumed children, who excitedly went from vehicle to vehicle "trunk or treating", collecting candy and goodies. After their sacks were full, everyone was treated to a free meal of hot dogs, chips, and apple cider. The afternoon wrapped up with awards for best costume and best "trunk". The smiles on all of the faces made it clear that everyone, young and old, would be looking forward to joining the fun again the following year.

The beginning for 2008 brought some sprucing up around the Hammock. In January, the tennis courts were given a much needed facelift. Additionally, after several fund-raising campaigns, a new pistol range building was constructed on the 25-yard line and three concrete benches were installed at the rifle range on the 100-yard line. Thanks to the equestrians who volunteered their time, talent, and cash, the riding arena was lit-up in 2008.

In April 2008, the new Indian Hammock community website was announced. The website was given the dedicated domain name of ihammock.net, with volunteer, Carol Devine acting as the webmaster under the direct supervision of the manager.

At the April board meeting, a unanimous vote was taken to reinstate the resident deputy program. This time the deputy would be offered the bunkhouse as his complimentary housing.

Spring activities over at the Skeet & Trap field included a Tombstone Shoot and an American Skeet Championship. The Tombstone Shoot was won by both Bob Morrison and Ray LaChapelle, who tied each other. The American Skeet Championship winners were Al Weidenfeller, Bob Benz, and Gus Roberts. Over in the ladies' division, the winners were Janice Whiting and Darb Behrens.

Beginning on May 1, 2008, the gate was staffed around-the-clock on Fridays and Saturdays for a 90-day trial. The current staff of attendants continued covering the daytime hours with the weekend nights covered by ICON Security Services. On June 15, John Lynch provided the membership with an update on the service. The number of cars entering the gate per night was only 34 and most of those were members. At the conclusion of the trial, the night gate coverage was terminated.

Hurricane season preparations began in the early summer. The community had mastered early preparations since 2004 when Charlie, Frances, and Jeanne blew through Indian Hammock. Although the 2008 season was a relatively quiet one, Indian Hammock did receive a deluge from

Tropical Storm Faye.   After her trip through the Caribbean, Faye skirted up the Florida west coast on August 18 and 19. Although spared the brunt of her tropical force strength winds, Okeechobee was hit by what is known as the "wet side of the storm".   By the morning of August 20, the rains had subsided enough for everyone to venture out to assess the damage.   At the board meeting on September 21, John Lynch reported that Indian Hammock had never seen flooding like this in its 35-year history. The standing water had been up to two feet deep in some areas and the power had been out for 18 hours.   Fortunately, no homes were damaged by winds or flooding.

2008 Tropical Storm Faye flooding

In October 2008, the skeet and trap range was renamed the "George Arata Shotgun Sports Complex" in honor of George's 20-plus years of time, commitment, and knowledge shared with the Skeet and Trap enthusiasts.

PART TWO
The History of Fort Drum

When you hear the words "ghost town", what comes to mind? Somewhere out west? Possibly Arizona or New Mexico? Maybe you close your eyes and see a locale with tumbleweeds tumbling down dirt roads and can almost hear the sound of wind whistling through vacant wood buildings. Well, I have good news for you.

You do not need to go any further than right outside our gate to visit a real ghost town. According to Albert DeVane of Lake Placid, Florida, an accomplished historical and genealogical researcher, Fort Drum is described as one of Florida's ghost towns. So, let's look back at the town before it was left to the ghosts, reviewing some of the history, the reason for settling, and the lifestyle of the early pioneers when they settled right here in Fort Drum.

Our history lesson begins at the end of the Second Seminole War. In 1842, the U.S. Army built a network of forts across the central part of the state, with military roads connecting them. Of those roads, one was roughly an east-west road running from Fort Basinger to Fort Vinton, which was located north of present-day Vero Beach. The other road ran approximately north-south from Fort Kissimmee to Fort Jupiter, and came to be known as the 'old wire road'. Where the two roads crossed is where Fort Drum was built. The U.S. Army used the fort for only a short time and then abandoned it in 1861.

Settlers began to make their way here in the 1870's, after the Civil War. The area was considered excellent cattle country. The first pioneer in Fort Drum was Henry Parker, who moved to the area in 1873. He built a double-pen log home and a store/trading post. The Seminole Indians would be regular customers. Parker sold them groceries, supplies, guns, and ammunition in exchange for alligator, deer, and otter hides, alligator teeth, and bird plumes, and also coontie flour, which was used by the pioneers for starch and cooking.

Nineteenth century Fort Drum social life consisted of political picnics, square dances, fish fries, cane grindings, candy pulls, and camp outs. The new settlers moving to the area were mainly cattlemen, farmers, and hunters. The town began to boom, building a church, school, blacksmith shop, and shoe and saddle shop. A short time later, Henry Parker was elected to the state legislature and while in Tallahassee, he promised a post office for Fort Drum. The government soon after made the award and he was named postmaster.

With the establishment of Fort Pierce's "St. Lucie County Tribune" in 1905, Fort Drum news was reported on a regular basis in the early issues of that newspaper. The following are some of the items appearing in the Tribune.

> October 27, 1905 - The stockowners here have been very busy this past week cow hunting. This is their last hunt 'til spring. They report plenty of water on the ground.

> October 27, 1905 - J. W. Knight and G. W. Drawdy while out riding Wednesday afternoon surprised an eight-foot alligator on the edge of a swamp, in water two or three feet deep. They fired at it with a shotgun and apparently killed it, but when they caught it by the nose, oh my, you should have seen it throw the water.

Another well directed shot put an end to its struggles, and they were able to drag it to shore.

November 24, 1905 - J. W. Knight killed the largest wild cat ever brought to Fort Drum.

December 21, 1906 - Outside of a few hunting parties and perhaps a dance, Christmas will be dull in Fort Drum this year.

The Kissimmee Valley Extension of the Florida East Coast Railroad (FEC) was completed through Fort Drum in 1914. A small depot was built at Fort Drum and, several miles north, another station was established and given the name Osowaw. Some five miles southeast of Fort Drum, the railroad constructed a station and gave it the name Hilolo. Both Osowaw and Hilolo are today also listed as ghost towns.

Fort Drum continued to prosper until the 1929 stock market crash and the subsequent Great Depression. In 1929, the FEC declared bankruptcy. Although they reemerged in 1931, the FEC shut down many of their lines, including those that ran through Fort Drum. With the loss of the railroad, residents and businesses began leaving Fort Drum and hence the moniker of "ghost town".

Although Fort Drum is listed as a ghost town, its people share a love for rural country living that makes them self-reliant and hearty.

PART THREE
The History of Okeechobee

CHAPTER ONE
The First Settlers

We take a step back in time once again and visit the city we now call Okeechobee and learn about some of its pioneers.

Our trip starts in October 1896 when Peter and Louisiana Raulerson, along with their children, moved to the area a few miles north of Lake Okeechobee in what was then still Saint Lucie County. They were the first permanent pioneer settlers in this yet unnamed area. Upon arriving, Peter stretched miles of fence from Taylor Creek to the Kissimmee River to contain his cattle. Shortly afterward, he named the area "The Bend" because the settlement was at the bend of the shorelines of Taylor Creek and the Kissimmee River.

The first school was constructed in The Bend in 1898. It was just a cabbage palmetto shack with the floors made of wood and the seats made from split timbers. Six children were required to start a school and since The Bend only had four students, two children were "borrowed" from Platt's Bluff on the Kissimmee River in order to achieve the required enrollment. The schoolteacher for the first term was Dr. George Hubbard, a Connecticut Yankee who moved to the area just before the school was opened. The children used to laugh and call him "Old Mother Hubbard" after the nursery rhyme. Louisiana Raulerson provided room and board to the teacher and to the extra students.

The school term was only four months long because the students were required to help at home planting gardens, tending to the cattle, and working other necessary jobs. It was joked at the time that the students enjoyed attending school more than their "vacation time".

The third schoolteacher for the community of The Bend was Tantie Huckaby, who was a well-educated woman originally from South Carolina. Tantie was a white-haired prim lady, who was well-known in the community for encouraging her students to strive for excellence. Her story may have ended there, except that she was instrumental in giving the area its second name.

The citizens of The Bend decided mail service was needed, so with the assistance of Robert LaMartin of Basinger, the Raulersons obtained permission for a post office, which was formally established on April 24, 1902. Ms. Huckaby asked that the new post office be named for her, and so it and the town were designated "Tantie".

The first postmaster was Mattie R. Walker, the daughter of Peter Raulerson. She served until June 7, 1902, when her father was appointed postmaster. The post office was located in the Raulerson home with the mail kept in a box under Louisiana Raulerson's bed. Mail was first carried between Tantie and Fort Drum on horseback by Peter Raulerson on what was known as a star route. A star route was a postal delivery route served by a private contractor. (Today, it is known as a highway contract route). Peter Raulerson carried the mail weekly for eighteen months without compensation.

The year was 1903 and although women still did not have the right to vote, the town of Tantie had seven male residents prepared to vote in the 1904 presidential election. Pioneer resident and judge, Henry Hancock, was instrumental in establishing the first voting precinct for Tantie that year.

In 1905 Lewis Raulerson, son of Peter and Louisiana, became the town's first merchant. He built his home and store at the location of present-day Parrott Avenue and Southeast Fourth Street. The location was conveniently near Taylor Creek, where supply boats would arrive. Once his business was established, he moved the post office from his parents' home to the store. In 1906, Lewis Raulerson was appointed the postmaster.

After the turn of the century, the catfish industry grew rapidly. In 1906, Captain Tom Bass turned catfishing in Tantie into a large-scale operation, in part due to his 56-foot steamer, named "Success", built by Harmon Raulerson. The steamer could carry 6000 pounds of catfish from Lake Okeechobee to Fort Myers. Captain Bass operated the successful Okeechobee Fish and Fur Company, prompting many catfish camps to crop up along the lake shoreline.

In 1909, the first official schoolhouse was built. It was designated "School 14" by the Saint Lucie County school system. School 14 was a one-story structure located on Parrott Avenue. The enrollment for the 1909-1910 school year was 31 students, including fourteen Raulerson and seven Hancock children. This structure is now re-located to Hwy 98 near the airport as part of the Okeechobee Historical Society and Museum.

Early pioneers in Tantie received medical care from teacher and physician, Dr. Hubbard, and from Merida Drawdy Raulerson, wife of William Raulerson, who moved to Tantie from Kissimmee. Merida would charge $10 dollars for each baby delivered, but was rarely paid in cash; acceptance of a chicken as payment was more common.

In 1911, doctors Roy and Anna Darrow arrived in Tantie. Both came to Florida and had recently passed their medical school exams. Anna had the distinction of attaining a 98%, the highest score in history on the exam, and the second woman ever licensed as a doctor in Florida. Dr. Roy ran the "Park Drugs" pharmacy, which was built next to Raulerson's store. Dr. Roy also did surgery on both humans and animals.

Dr. Anna, affectionately referred to as "Doc Anna" became somewhat of a legend in Tantie, practicing for 10 years and charging $1 for an office visit. She drove all over in her Model T treating patients wherever there was a need. Regardless of her patient's social status, the hour of the day, or the distance she had to drive, Doc Anna would be there. When babies were delivered, Doc Anna would travel with Merida, training her to become a midwife. Together, they improved the standards of hygiene for childbirth. Upon completion of her training with Doc Anna, Merida was certified as a midwife and continued to work for 40 years with every doctor who came to town.

CHAPTER TWO
Railroad Brings Growth

On December 30, 1910, exciting news came to the sleepy little village. The president of the FEC Railroad, J. R. Parrott, announced that Mr. Flagler had approved construction of a rail line to the northern edge of the lake. This prompted the first big boom for the area from 1911 to 1919.

Along with the railroad came a new name for the community. The name Tantie was deemed inappropriate for this city with so much potential, so on October 4, 1911, the post office of Tantie was officially changed to Okeechobee, using the name already in use for the lake. The name Okeechobee comes from the Hitchiti language of the Seminole Tribe, oki (water) and chubi (big). At around the same time, James Ingraham, a vice president of the FEC and primary architect of the project, was credited with coining the name "The Chicago of Florida" when referring to Okeechobee.

In 1912, the excitement of the railroad picked up momentum prompting the arrival of major land companies to the area. Land sales were brisk. The FEC formed the Model Land Company, which laid out the City of Okeechobee, including naming the main north-south street after Mr. Parrott. The Model Land Company also donated large plats of land to several religious denominations including the: Baptist, Church of God, Catholic, Methodist, and Episcopal churches. Several of the churches still stand today on the land that was so graciously donated. Mr. Ingraham of the FEC also formed the Okeechobee Land

Company with FEC employee, W. L. Bragg, who moved to Okeechobee to sell lots and farm sites.

By July 1912, the work on the railroad was underway and finally, in the predawn hours of January 4, 1915, the first passenger train arrived in Okeechobee. Then, on June 4 of that same year, the City of Okeechobee was incorporated by a special act of the Florida Legislature. The governor appointed Peter Raulerson as the first mayor of the new city. The council members also appointed by the governor included Lewis Raulerson and Dr. Darrow, along with three other early pioneers of the area.

On July 1, 1915, the *Okeechobee Call*, the town's first newspaper, was established. The editor of the weekly paper was George T. Rice, who moved to Okeechobee in early 1915. The Call was printed in Fort Pierce by A. K. Wilson.

The first council meeting was held at 8 pm on July 13, 1915 with the following motions voted on and approved: setting dates for future meetings, selecting a police chief, and designing a city seal. Council meetings were fixed for the first Tuesday of the month at 7:30 pm. A meeting was set for July 14th at 4 pm to consider Chief of Police applications.

On July 14, the council met and decided that the city seal would include the words "City of Okeechobee" and a monogram described as "a lake and a boat with the sail hoisted". This meeting finally adjourned on July 15th in the wee hours of the morning.

The first council meetings ushered in a day of celebrating the new town. The day included foot and horse races, a greased pole contest, a baseball game, a musical program, and a fish fry.

Following the incorporation of the City of Okeechobee, the new city felt its largest boom to date. The fishing businesses, trapping businesses, cattle ranches, and the rapidly growing timber and turpentine industries drew many new businesses to the area. Each new arrival was anxious to live in, and open their business in, the highly touted "Chicago of Florida". It was during 1915 that Okeechobee welcomed the following businesses: a second pharmacy, a bakery, a barbershop, a hardware and furniture store, a lumber company and sawmill, a feed store, two hotels, a blacksmith, a dairy, several taverns, a bank, and Raulerson's new department store.

Along with the increase in population, Okeechobee saw its fair share of lawlessness, likely making the job of the top lawman for the city a difficult task. The history books, along with anecdotal stories from the time, describe an ongoing friction between the catfisherman and the ranch cowboys. It is reported that on their off-time while visiting the town taverns, many fights broke out between the rival gangs.

The first Chief of Police (City Marshal) for the new city was Benjamin F. Hall, selected on July 14, 1915; however, he only served until September of that year. Then on October 12, 1915, J. W. Raulerson was selected as the second marshal and held the office until March 14, 1916. On that day, the council appointed William E. Collins, also known as "Pogy Bill", to the position. He was arguably one of the more memorable characters and most successful law officers for this emerging city.

CHAPTER THREE
Pogy Bill

William E. Collins was born on an unnamed American cargo vessel on May 24, 1884 while the ship was docked at the harbor in Sydney, Australia. According to maritime law, even though not born in the USA, he was an American citizen. With his parents, he spent most of his childhood and teen years on one ship or another, making long runs around the southern tip of South America.

The rigors of ship life were harsh for a full-grown adult, but for a child the hardship could be nearly insurmountable; however, Bill survived and even thrived. This may possibly explain his toughness later in life. It was during his shipboard life that he learned to fight to keep everything he had, regardless of how meager. Shipboard life tended to be lawless and because of his youth, the crewmembers considered him an easy target. It was during this time that he learned that he could earn money by fighting and he became quite a formidable opponent, even to men several years his senior.

By the time Bill was in his early twenties, he was just over six feet tall with short legs and longer trunk and arms. This stature gave him what is considered the perfect boxer's build, tall but with a low center of gravity. It was reported in stories that have endured over the years that Bill could drive his fist through an inch-thick oak plank, thanks to loading cargo all day and pit-fighting in the ship's hold at night.

In 1905, when Bill was 21 years old, he reportedly jumped ship in Buenos Aires and stowed away until he reached Florida, where the ship docked in Tampa. Tampa at the time was the gateway to the great-untamed wilderness of south-central Florida.

Bill quickly found work in Tampa as a boilermaker and it was here he got his first taste of politics through his experience with the labor unions. As a boilermaker, Bill found himself caught up in territorial disputes and brawls almost daily, as was common with opposing gangs of laborers, and he loved every minute of it. Since fist fighting in the labor unions was the way of establishing territory, Bill soon became a thorn in the side of rival gangs because no one could beat him in a fight.

It was 1910 when a rival gang pooled their money and hired a professional prizefighter to face Bill; however, it only took five rounds for Bill to knock his opponent unconscious, which further infuriated the group. It was shortly after this fight that Bill packed up and moved to Tantie. There are two possible reasons cited for his decision to move, one being that he was hoping to find a place of adventure with no one to tell him what to do. The second was that he might have been looking for a place to hide from the gang he had just infuriated. Regardless of the reason, his historic stay in Okeechobee was about to begin.

Upon arriving in Tantie, he joined a fishing camp and soon became a leader of the local fishermen. It was while he worked at the fishing camp that he received the nickname of Pogy Bill. After a particularly bad day of fishing, he returned to camp and found the game warden waiting for him. Embarrassed that he had no catch that day, he handed over his bait bag hoping that the agent would not check the contents. However, the agent did and when he opened the bag he exclaimed, "There ain't nothin' in here but pogies." Pogies, for those not familiar with the term, are freshwater baitfish not edible by humans. From that day forward, William Collins became known as Pogy Bill.

In the early days of Okeechobee, the weekends were a time when both the catfisherman and cowboys headed into town for some libation, and trouble always seemed to follow.

There already was a rivalry between both groups, with Pogy Bill considered the leader of the fishermen. Of course, with the liquor in the mix, things frequently got out of hand, ultimately causing the business owners to appeal to Judge Hancock to stop the mischief once and for all. Judge Hancock promised the community that the next time Pogy Bill was in town, Bill would be shown no mercy and would stand before the bar of justice.

When Pogy Bill received word of Judge Hancock's promise, Pogy sent word back that if the judge attempted to arrest him, he would "dump the judge in the lake", and many believed that he would do it. Judge Hancock deputized a group of men that included some of the toughest cowhunters in the area. On Pogy Bill's next trip into town, he was arrested and locked up in a railroad boxcar used as a makeshift jail cell.

The following morning, Pogy Bill was brought into the courtroom, which was in the back of Darrow's Drug Store. Bill's mood was obviously very sour from spending the night inside a steaming hot boxcar. Once court was called to order, Judge Hancock found Pogy Bill guilty of a laundry list of skullduggery charges. Bill watched as the judge flipped through the thick paperback statue book pondering the stiffness of the sentence he was about to impose. After a few minutes, Pogy Bill blurted out, "I ain't gonna be charged out of no g**d**** Sears and Roebuck Catalog". The outburst did not sit well with the judge who promptly added $25 to the fines and sentenced Pogy Bill to 90 days in the Fort Pierce jail.

Fortunately for Pogy Bill, many of the town's people, including Doc Anna, knew that he was truly a good man, so she traveled to the county seat in Ft. Pierce to talk to Judge Hancock about commuting the sentence. Judge Hancock listened to her pleading and then spoke personally to Pogy Bill, making him promise to give up his lawless ways. Pogy Bill agreed, was released, and never broke his promise to the judge.

On March 14, 1916, not long after his turnaround, William "Pogy Bill" Collins became the third marshal for the City of Okeechobee and the first who was successful in taming this rough and tough town.

In late March 1917, community leaders in Okeechobee met and decided to press for the formation of a new county. After the bill passed through the Florida Legislature, Okeechobee County officially came into being on May 8, 1917, although the law did not take effect until August 7, 1917.

The first Okeechobee County Sheriff was Smith J. Drawdy, who died in office after succumbing to the flu in 1918. Pogy Bill became the next sheriff and stayed in the position for 13 years.

When Bill began his walk on the lawful side, his life-change was not limited to his role as marshal and sheriff. He was also well-known for supporting the youth of the county. He was credited with starting a youth baseball team. He also bought many of the boys boxing gloves and taught them how to box. He also started a Boy Scout troop. He intuitively knew that the youth of the community needed an outlet for their emotions and energy in order to keep them on the straight and narrow.

Bill married Ebbie Merle Dupree (1905-1992) in the 1920's, but the couple never had any children. Pogy Bill's kindness and concern was not limited to the youth of the community, who he considered his adopted children. Many stories are still told to this day of the kindness he showed to those in need. Many times he literally gave his last penny to someone in need, bought a barefoot child a new pair of shoes, brought food to a family who would otherwise go hungry, or would make sure an employer would pay his worker the wages earned.

The outlaw Pogy Bill was now the lawman and philanthropist Pogy Bill, but prohibition was enacted in 1920 and things began to change.

In the 1920's and prohibition is now the law of the land. Although Pogy Bill had quit drinking many years before, he saw no harm in a person having a drink.

Also at this point in Okeechobee history, the once thriving businesses were now struggling. The fishing business was no longer a profitable enterprise, the existing cattle businesses required fewer employees, and the woods were almost hunted out. The only thriving industry was lumber, but the local sawmill brought in labor from outside of Okeechobee. Pogy Bill was keenly aware that a great number of Okeechobee residents derived their only income from making and selling moonshine. Due to the dense undergrowth around the lake, with scrubs and hammocks, the area was ideal for setting up and concealing stills.

When a large still was located and reported to Sheriff Pogy Bill, he always responded that he would get around to investigating it, but typically never did and really just looked the other way. He was acutely aware of his community and knew many people depended on this industry for their livelihood. On the other hand, he did not let the moonshiners run wild. In his usual Pogy Bill style, he supervised the illegal activities according to his own code. Unfortunately, his system did not exactly comply with federal regulations, and Pogy Bill found himself under investigation.

In the northeast section of town, the tracks for the St. Andrews Bay Lumber Company trains ran right past a still. Allegedly unknown to the officials of the lumber company, the trains had been hauling in sugar and meal and then hauling out the moonshine in barrels, concealed under the piles of lumber. On one of the shipments heading north, the concealed cargo sprang a leak while in the railroad yards in

Lake Wales. Government agents were called in and launched a thorough investigation of the crime. While they were not able to find sufficient evidence to charge Pogy Bill with manufacturing the moonshine, they did charge the sheriff and one of his deputies with guarding the road while the illegal booze was being loaded onto the train.

The sheriff was tried twice in the federal court in Miami. The first trial ended in a hung jury. The second jury found Bill guilty on three counts of conspiracy, each carrying a two-year prison sentence. He appealed the conviction, and although the original verdict was upheld, he was placed on six years probation .

Bill resigned from the office of sheriff. However, his resignation was not the result of public pressure; rather, he wanted to save Gov. Doyle C. Carleton embarrassment. In fact, the Okeechobee community sent the governor a petition urging the governor not to accept the resignation. Seven hundred residents, representing about 90 percent of the county voters at that time, signed the petition.

In 1933, Pogy Bill ran again for sheriff, and for the first time in his political career, he was defeated, but only by four votes. Shortly after the election, he took a job in Indiantown for a brief time, then accepted the chief of police position in Frostproof, Florida. He also served as a volunteer firefighter for the city.

In February 1935, while on his way to a fire, an accident left Bill pinned under an overturned fire truck. He appeared unhurt at the time, but developed pneumonia and died 3 days later. Pogy Bill is buried in the Evergreen Cemetery in Okeechobee.

CHAPTER FOUR
Calamities

Before we ever heard of Frances, Jean, Camille, Andrew, and Katrina, in fact before hurricanes were named, came one of the top five deadliest hurricanes of all time. This nameless terror, still known today only as the 1928 Okeechobee Hurricane, left its mark on the area surrounding Lake Okeechobee. The storm dramatically impacted the early pioneers, changed the topography of the lakeshore, and was the catalyst for change in storm preparations for non-coastal areas.

In the early 1920's, when the total population around Lake Okeechobee reached about 2,000, the state constructed an earthen 47-mile-long levee, with a 40-foot base and a 5-to-9-foot height, along the southern shoreline to protect residents and their crops from flooding. Nevertheless, in 1926, although not a direct hit on Okeechobee, the Great Miami Hurricane pounded the area with hurricane-force wind speeds and pushed the lake waters over the levee, destroying homes and farms and killing over 150 people. Hit especially hard was the town of Moore Haven. For the next two years, the Everglades farmers lobbied the Florida Legislature for state funds to repair and expand the levee. However, each time the bill was voted down. With no other options, the residents just hoped that they would be spared from another hurricane. Unfortunately, in 1928 their fears were realized.

The storm of 1928, like most hurricanes, formed off the coast of Africa and meandered across the Atlantic Ocean picking up moisture and wind velocity. The hurricane made stops of destruction along the way in Guadeloupe on September 12 and then the Virgin Islands before making a direct hit on

Puerto Rico where more than 300 lives were lost. Without weakening, the storm continued its tirade striking the Bahamas on September 14 and 15 before heading for the U.S. coast. The eyewall made landfall near Jupiter, arriving as what would be categorized today as a category 4 hurricane, bringing with it a 10-foot storm surge and crashing into the barrier islands with waves estimated at 20-feet high.

Before 1928, hurricanes were predicted to weaken when they marched over land; however, this storm defied previous predictions and remained a major hurricane as it pushed its way inland with the eye on a direct path to Lake Okeechobee. The residents of the towns around Lake Okeechobee battened down in their homes, with many generations gathering under one roof. As the hurricane churned closer to the U.S. coast, the animals gave their telltale warnings signals; flocks of wading birds disappeared towards the horizon, no birds were flying, cattle laid low in the fields, fish schools moved to deeper waters in the lakes and canals. The native Seminoles watched the wildlife transition, heeded their warning, and headed for higher ground.

At 6:45 in the evening on September 16, 1928, the skies over Lake Okeechobee turned ominously dark as if to predict a disaster approaching that none of the pioneers could imagine. Then shortly before midnight, the storm arrived ushered in by winds that were estimated at 150-mph. The waters of Lake Okeechobee began churning like a pot of boiling stew. The meager dikes were no match for the storm surge, and within minutes, they were breached sending a wall of water into the areas around the south and north parts of the lake. As homes were swept off their foundations, families scurried to their rooftops only to be violently tussled by the floodwaters. Only the strong were able to withstand the jarring on these makeshift rafts. The floodwaters reached a level of 20 feet, not receding for almost a week.

After finishing its destruction, the storm moved on a northward course through the center of Florida, then continued its trek along the coastlines of Georgia, South Carolina, North Carolina, and Virginia before finally dissipating to a tropical wave over Pennsylvania. With the floods finally receding, the survivors along Lake Okeechobee slowly started emerging to assess the damage and loss of life. Although there was flooding north of the lake covering the City of Okeechobee, it quickly became painfully clear that the flood damage had more severely impacted the towns to the south. Most heavily hit were the towns of Pahokee, Canal Point, Chosen, Belle Glade, and South Bay.

On Tuesday morning, September 18, thirty-six hours after the hurricane's arrival, newspapers around the nation summarized the calamity with headlines reading, "Florida Destroyed! Florida Destroyed!" Very few relief agencies rushed to the aid of the survivors around Lake Okeechobee. In fact, most attention was directed at the destruction along the coast. However, word soon spread of the great disaster around the lake, the scope of which would take many days to realize. Dead bodies, both human and animal, were scattered everywhere, decomposing in the Florida sun with each passing day. Many of those who had managed to survive had been swept with the floodwaters deep into the sawgrass and were forced to walk or wade back miles to any recognizable roadway they could find. Some, too weak or injured to stand or walk, sat for days in hopes of being spotted by passersby. Some who survived the storm are believed to have perished later as they wandered the vast Everglades.

Although the exact number of those who perished in the Okeechobee storm will never be ascertained, the accepted number in the history books is listed as over 2500. Approximately three-fourths or more of those casualties were non-white migrant workers, many of whom had come from the Bahama Islands. Accounting for their numbers was complicated by their migratory habits and the fact that most of them were known, even to their friends, only by a nickname.

Coffins were brought in by the truckload, bringing with them the sickening reality of the lives lost. With no place to bury the dead, two mass graves were dug to accomplish segregation in death just as it had been in life during that time. Sixteen hundred whites were buried in a mass grave at Port Mayaca and 674 black victims were buried in a mass grave in a pauper's field in West Palm Beach. It wasn't until 80 years after the storm that plaques were erected at both sites honoring those who perished.

The River and Harbor Act of 1930 authorized the construction of levees for 67.8 miles along the south shore of the lake and 15.7 miles along the north shore. The U. S. Army Corps of Engineers constructed the levees between 1932 and 1937, named the Herbert Hoover Dike. A major hurricane in 1947 prompted the need for additional flood and storm damage reduction work. Subsequently, Congress passed the Flood Control Act of 1948 authorizing a comprehensive plan to provide flood and storm damage reduction. As a result, a new dike system was completed in the late 1960's. The dike system, which still stands today, consists of 143 miles of levee with 19 culverts, hurricane gates, and other water control structures.

Although the late 1920's were a time of disasters, starting with the land sale bust and followed immediately by two devastating hurricanes, things were going to get worse before they got better.

In 1929, with post hurricane clean up and rebuilding still in full swing, the pioneers were challenged by another unwelcome guest. In April of that year, a Mediterranean fruit fly infestation started in grapefruit trees in rural Central Florida and spread throughout Florida. The infestation destroyed about 60 percent of the entire fruit production in the state. An embargo on citrus fruit was imposed and tons of fruit were destroyed. Soon after the discovery, an eradication program was established that included massive tree cutting throughout the state. The Florida fruit fly infestation of 1929 was the most costly infestation in state history, costing over 7 million dollars. That equates to just over 95 million dollars in today's dollars.

In October of that year, as the fruit fly continued its rampage, Okeechobee and the entire nation fell victims to the Great Depression. Although the town lost several business and banks with the resulting loss of jobs, a couple of businesses survived and even thrived during this difficult time. We will look at two of Okeechobee's bright spots that emerged during these dark times, the cattle industry and Markham Brothers Canning Plant.

Despite the Great Depression, the cattle industry continued to increase in importance in the 1930's. The 40,000 head of cattle in Okeechobee County in 1920 had dropped to approximately 15,000 by 1928, but by 1938 their numbers had grown once again to a total of 35,000 head, under the ownership of 156 different ranchers. Besides just an increase in the quantity of cattle, the quality of the cattle gradually improved due to tick eradication and the introduction of purebred bulls. The Okeechobee County Cattlemen's Association was organized in 1937 with John Olan Pearce, Sr. serving as its first president.

In March 1939, the newspaper reported that the Okeechobee County Cattlemen's Association had begun construction on a livestock market, cattle shed, and pens. Then on May 5, 1939, the market opened, celebrating with an auction held before a large crowd. In July 1942, the Dixie Cattlemen's Association, a group of cattlemen operating as a large enterprise, took over ownership and management of the Cattle Auction Sales Ring in Okeechobee, and held sales every Thursday from July 9, 1942 until Dec. 21, 1942. During that period, they sold 3,512 head of cattle for a total of $113,763.51.

The other bright spot for Okeechobee was the Markham Brothers Canning Plant. What began as a family business in Homestead made its way to Okeechobee in 1938. Brothers, Allen and Roscoe Markham, followed in their grandfather and father's footsteps and started their own canning plant giving employment to many citizens of Okeechobee.

The City of Okeechobee gave the Markhams special water and tax rates to encourage them to start their cannery in the city. The brothers took advantage of the special rates and created optimism and prosperity for this city whose population at the time was just 1,500. Along with canned tomatoes, the plant produced ketchup and tomato juice. In no time, the plant was a success, employing over 100 people, mostly women, and producing up to 2,000 cases per day. The women employed by the plant were known to have said that if it weren't for the supplemental income from the cannery, they would not have been able to make ends meet with just their husbands' incomes.

The canning plant also provided free nursery care for their female employees' children, which filled a vital need after World War II started. Along with nursery care, the plant also offered housing for some workers.

In 1974, the plant had to close its doors. However, the men and women who worked for the company have fond memories and great appreciation for what the Markham brothers did for the economy of Okeechobee.

The cannery office building was located on Park Street, east of the cannery plant, in the building still standing today in the 600 block of SW Park Street. The cannery plant, which has since been torn down, was located west of the office, at the now vacant lot at the southeast corner of SW Park Street and SW 7th Avenue. Today, you can still see the large artesian well pipe that provided water to the cannery protruding above the ground.

While Okeechobee has grown in the past decades, it has maintained its small-town values and mystique. While some of the locals might not agree with that statement, having come from the big cities myself, I know my own soul appreciates the friendly and godly aura that is Okeechobee.

Made in the USA
Lexington, KY
09 November 2019